The Finger Game Miracle

Author
Nancy Kelton

Illustrator
Ron Recchio

🌳 Raintree Editions

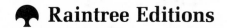

1 2 3 4 5 6 7 8 9 0   81 80 79 78 77

Library of Congress Number: 76-46408
Printed in the United States of America.

Published by   ♠ **Raintree Editions**
                        A Division of Raintree Publishers Limited
                        Milwaukee, Wisconsin 53203

Distributed by   Childrens Press
                        1224 West Van Buren Street
                        Chicago, Illinois 60607

Library of Congress Cataloging in Publication Data

Kelton, Nancy.
   The finger game miracle.

   SUMMARY: A biography of Helen Keller who overcame her
handicap with the help of teacher Anne Sullivan.
   1. Keller, Helen Adams, 1880-1968—Juvenile
literature. 2. Blind-deaf—Biography—Juvenile
literature. 3. Blind—United States—Biography—
Juvenile literature. [1. Keller, Helen Adams, 1880-1968.
2. Blind-deaf. 3. Physically handicapped] 1. Title.
HV1624.K4K45   362.4'092'4 [B]   76-46408
ISBN 0-8172-0452-0 lib. bdg.

For My Mother

The Finger Game Miracle

A True Story About Helen Keller

6

Helen was not like other children. When she was a baby, she had a very serious illness which left her blind, deaf, and dumb. All the words she was beginning to understand and all the sounds she was beginning to babble lost their meaning. Her happy little world turned into a dark, silent one since neither the loudest noises nor the brightest lights could reach her.

The older she got, the naughtier she behaved. She broke her toys and pushed the furniture around. She threw her food around the room and ate with her hands. Whenever her mother tried to comb her hair or change her clothes, Helen kicked her or pushed her away. Much of the time she looked and behaved more like an animal than a person.

8

Helen's parents were afraid to punish her, and every day they faced another battle. Helen became increasingly difficult to handle. Her parents wrote letters to hospitals and spoke to doctors from all over the country, but no one had any answers.

One day Helen's mother read a newspaper article about a special school called the Perkins Institute where teachers were trained to work with handicapped children. She wrote a letter and arranged to have a teacher come to their home.

Late one afternoon, a young woman named Miss Sullivan arrived in a carriage. Helen's parents rushed out to greet her while the little girl stood on the porch trying to figure out what all the fuss was about. Miss Sullivan noticed Helen immediately and walked over to her. Helen felt footsteps coming closer and closer. As soon as the stranger was near enough, Helen kicked her in the knee. Then she grabbed Miss Sullivan's suitcase and ran inside. Miss Sullivan chased after her and found her in the guest room opening up the bag.

"What a curious little monkey you are!" she said with a smile. "You're just dying to learn. We might as well begin."

11

Helen found a box of candy under the clothes and opened it. Miss Sullivan took it away. Helen frowned. No one ever took things away from her. Helen hit the stranger. Much to her surprise, the stranger immediately hit her back. This made Helen angry. She started to run out of the room, but Miss Sullivan grabbed her.

Then Miss Sullivan did something strange. She took the little girl's hand and made curious shapes into it with her own fingers. The shapes were letters. Miss Sullivan was spelling candy.

Miss Sullivan played the finger game again and again. C-a-n-d-y, c-a-n-d-y she wrote. Helen sat very still. What was this person doing?

13

Miss Sullivan offered her palm to Helen. The little girl made the exact same shapes into her hand. When she completed the word, the teacher gave her a piece of chocolate. Miss Sullivan put Helen's hand to her face and nodded her head up and down to show she was pleased.

At dinner that evening, Helen walked around the table taking bread and potatoes from her parents' plates; and, as usual, they ignored her. When she got to Miss Sullivan's place, she started to take her roll. Miss Sullivan grabbed it back. Helen took it again, and Miss Sullivan hit her.

Helen's mother rose to her feet.

"Miss Sullivan," she said, "you must let her do what she wants. We've never been able to stop her."

Miss Sullivan was holding Helen's hands firmly, keeping them away from her plate.

14

15

"I'm going to put an end to this nonsense," she said. Helen was squirming, and Miss Sullivan tightened her grasp. "You treat her as if she were your pet. She has to learn that other people have rights before she can learn anything else."

The rest of the meal turned into a wrestling match. When Helen dropped her napkin, Miss Sullivan made her pick it up. When she picked up her lettuce with her fingers, Miss Sullivan placed a fork in her hand. When she tried to run after her parents, who had left the room because they couldn't bear to watch the fight, the teacher forced her back into her seat. Eventually, Helen was too tired and hungry to fight. She gave in to the stranger.

This struggle at the dinner table
was not their last. Each day brought
new battles. Both Helen and Miss
Sullivan were often too exhausted to
accomplish anything else.

Miss Sullivan realized that as long as Helen's parents were around, she would not be able to teach Helen anything. Being alone with her was the only answer. Miss Sullivan knew that Helen's parents owned a little unoccupied cottage down the road, and she asked their permission to take Helen there. At first they refused. They were afraid to let Helen go. Helen had never been away from them before. When they realized how important it was for them to cooperate, they finally agreed to let Miss Sullivan take her—but only for two weeks.

The next morning, Helen and her teacher took a carriage ride to the cottage. The smell of the flowers along the way made Helen smile. She loved being outdoors.

19

When they arrived at their new
home and she realized that her mother
and father were nowhere around,

Helen started misbehaving again. She refused to eat dinner. When Miss Sullivan finally got her into bed after a long, hard struggle, she slept all the way over to one side as far away from the teacher as she could be.

Little by little, she learned to mind Miss Sullivan. It became clear that she couldn't have her way with her teacher, who was so much stronger than she was. Helen began to see that this woman was not her enemy after all.

They played the finger game all the time. Every time Helen touched something new, Miss Sullivan would spell a word into her hand, and Helen would spell it right back. Even though she knew that she was doing something right by imitating Miss Sullivan, Helen still had no idea what all those funny shapes meant.

Helen learned to use her fork properly, and when her teacher put a napkin under her chin, she left it there. She even learned how to knit. Sometimes she would sit quietly for hours in a big rocking chair with her needles and yarn. Helen and Miss Sullivan took long walks together and picked flowers. They even played the funny finger game outside.

When Helen's parents arrived at the end of two weeks, they were delighted with her progress. Miss Sullivan was not nearly as happy.

"We've done a lot," she told them, "but Helen still doesn't understand that these finger games mean something. If we had more time alone, I think I could teach her that."

"We made a deal," said Helen's father. "Now it's time to come home."

23

Everything was fine for the next few days, and Helen seemed happy to be home. But one morning something peculiar happened. Helen woke up feeling particularly cross. Miss Sullivan played the finger game, hoping it would put Helen in a better mood, but the game only made her angrier.

At breakfast Helen picked up an empty glass, and very quickly Miss Sullivan made the letters g-l-a-s-s in her free hand. Then she poured water into the glass and formed w-a-t-e-r.

Helen refused to spell either word. She just sat in her chair and frowned. Something was definitely bothering her. Why were two words spelled, one right after the other, in her hand? She started beating her fists on the table.

25

26

Miss Sullivan suddenly realized what was happening. Helen was bursting to get out of her locked cage and communicate. She wanted to know what those funny finger tricks meant.

Miss Sullivan grabbed an empty glass with one hand and Helen's arm with the other and dragged her outside to the pump.

She put the glass in one of Helen's hands and began pumping water into it while making w-a-t-e-r in her free hand.

W-a-t-e-r, w-a-t-e-r, w-a-t-e-r she spelled over and over.

Helen dropped the glass. It crashed to the ground and broke into little pieces. A light came into her eyes. As she felt the cold water rushing onto one hand and the shapes of the letters on the other, she knew that this liquid and the word went together.

Yes, that was it. That was what the finger tricks meant. They're words. Everything has a word. Every word means something.

Very quickly she spelled the word water into Miss Sullivan's hand and threw her arms around her. She patted the teacher's cheek, and Miss Sullivan made the letters t-e-a-c-h-e-r in her hand. Then Helen pointed to herself. H-e-l-e-n the teacher spelled. Helen smiled an enormous smile and jumped up and down. All the anger vanished from her face. For now she could communicate.

Within a short time, Helen knew hundreds of words and what they meant. Her parents learned the finger game too. Soon they were all spelling sentences to each other.

30

Eventually, Helen learned how to read and write books in Braille, the language of the blind. When she got a little older, she learned how to use her voice and began speaking all the words she had learned with her fingers.

After she graduated from school, Helen and Miss Sullivan traveled all over the world and made many wonderful friends. Helen Keller became famous throughout the world. She wrote beautiful books, gave speeches, and showed people who were blind and deaf that they could lead long, happy lives—just as she did.